Paul Beckwith left school at seventeen to go to hotel school. Graduating as a full member of the Hotel Catering and Institutional Management Association, he worked in various management roles prior to running his own restaurant with his wife, Mary.

Leaving this career behind, in 1984 Paul entered the life insurance industry and worked as a financial advisor, running his own independent financial advisory company.

After twenty years, he decided to 'retire' to spend more time on writing, consultancy and educating people in the intricacies – and yet simplicities – of the financial world that the Financial Services Authority has chosen to complicate and confuse.

Paul and Mary have two grown up daughters.

Picking Yourself Up
and Starting All Over Again

Picking Yourself Up and Starting All Over Again

Paul Beckwith

ATHENA PRESS
LONDON

Picking Yourself Up and Starting All Over Again
Copyright © Paul Beckwith 2006

All Rights Reserved

No part of this book may be reproduced in any form
by photocopying or by any electronic or mechanical means,
including information storage and retrieval systems,
without permission in writing from both the copyright
owner and the publisher of this book.

ISBN 1 84401 626 9

First Published 2006 by
ATHENA PRESS
Queen's House, 2 Holly Road
Twickenham TW1 4EG
United Kingdom

Printed for Athena Press

To all my friends at:
SOFA (Society of Financial Advisors)
LIA (Life Insurance Association)
MDRT (Million Dollar Round Table)

Also with thanks to Mary, my wife, and Amy and Sophie, my daughters, who have ever been my friends, proof readers and keenest supporters and critics

Disclaimer

We do not have the necessary deep pockets to pay the legal costs to put together the unreadable gobbledegook that lawyers would wrap around us to earn impossibly high fees, so I would warn you that this book is a set of ideas; my ideas to help you, the reader, improve your own financial circumstances.

We do not know each reader's personal financial situation, so we cannot give specific personal guidance. We are merely suggesting that it is your money and your life and you may want to change it for the better. However, we accept no liability for any of your personal actions.

Author's Note

> Pick yourself up,
> take a deep breath,
> dust yourself down
> and start all over again.
>
> Nothing's impossible, I have found,
> for when my chin is on the ground,
> I pick myself up,
> dust myself off,
> and start all over again.
>
> Don't lose your confidence
> if you slip,
> be grateful for a pleasant trip,
> and pick yourself up,
> dust yourself off,
> and start all over again.

So many people fall into the trap of spiralling debt, and once they have been sucked into this vortex, they often do not know how to get out!

This is a short guide to how to not just get out of debt but to stay out by using a little common sense and some easy-to-follow rules and ideas.

Not only will the reader be able to escape the spiral of debt, but they will be set in a position to amass savings and build a new financial world on a sound foundation.

This is an easy-to-read guide that is intended to help all kinds of people, whatever their circumstances and situations.

Not only will I help you to reduce your outgoings and debt, but I have also included some tips to increase your income and savings.

November 2005

Contents

Introduction: Is Debt a Burden?		15
1	Putting Your Finances in Order	17
	Do you Really want to put your Financial World in Order?	17
	Work with your Partner	18
2	Budgetary Control	20
3	Categorise and Review Your Expenditure	22
4	Assets, Liabilities and Debt Consolidation	26
5	Small and Subtle Changes	29
6	What Do You Want?	31
7	The Nitty Gritty	33
8	Credit Cards and Security	37
	A Cash-Spend Lifestyle	39
9	Redraw Your Budgets	40
10	Seek Professional Advice	45
	Specimen Questions	46
	The Cost of your Lifestyle: Your Mortgage	46
11	My Job	49
	Different Jobs	50
	Career Changes	51

12	Special Tools to Help You	53
	Mind Mapping	53
	Lateral Thinking	53
	Play It Forward	56
13	Avoid Bankruptcy	57
	Surviving Bankruptcy	57
	Voluntary Arrangement	59
	The Truth About Bankruptcy	60
	The Myths	61
14	Be a Winner	62
15	Summary	63
Appendix 1: Useful Contacts		66
Appendix 2: Synopsis of Money-saving Ideas		67
Appendix 3: Select Bibliography		68

Introduction
IS DEBT A BURDEN?

It's pay day.

You open your pay advice slip and your heart sinks. You feel physically sick. You know that the bank account is overdrawn and this pay packet does not even cover it. Worse still, the credit card payment is due next Tuesday and the mortgage next Friday. Still, you'll find a way, you lie to yourself. Then, just before you leave work, your bank manager rings. By the time he has finished berating you and telling you that you can no longer have that overdraft, you feel so sick you don't know what to do.

Well, I am here in this book to help you solve your problems.

No I am *not* a fairy godmother (I'm the wrong sex, to start with), but I do know how to help you help yourself. I know because I have been there, and I saw the light and made changes that had startling effects on my life for the better!

The first thing to do is to go home and sit down with your partner and talk to each other. You *must* make yourself a budget of your outgoings (expenses) and set these against your income. Then you will know by how much you are overspending. You have now made your first step towards solving your own financial problems!

Do not fall into the easy trap of blaming others for your own problems. Remember Jim Lovell's actions on Apollo Thirteen when his mission ran into trouble (possibly because his ship was built by the lowest bidder). He took full charge of the problem; he took *ownership* of it, acknowledging it in his message to Mission Control:

'Houston, we have a problem.'

Jim Lovell, his crew and Mission Control took ownership and solved that problem using ingenuity, lateral thinking and sheer guts and self belief. So be positive all the way through this book as well as life.

Remember: the glass jug is *not* half empty; *it is half full*!

Chapter 1
PUTTING YOUR FINANCES IN ORDER

Do you Really want to put your Financial World in Order?

Well, you appear to have taken the first step in stabilising your financial situation by buying my book. Please do take the time to read through the easy-to-follow steps and then take positive action. You have no idea how good you will feel at the end of each phase and, because I do want you to succeed, there are a series of rewards after each successfully completed stage. Just remember to stick at it so you too can say that you brushed yourself down, dusted yourself off and *started all over again*!

The first thing you need to do is to come to a complete agreement – with your partner, husband, wife, or even (if you are on your own) with yourself – that you are going to be serious about organising your financial future.

For instance:

- We are going to cut down on our daily expenses together.
- We are going to stop wasting money on useless purchases.
- I will make my own lunches for work instead of going out to the café/pub.
- We will grow our own produce.
- We will reduce our electricity and gas bills and also help save the planet.
- We will start this today!

It is no good going into this half-heartedly! That will actually cause you more heartache and problems than you could believe. So agree on a course of action, and – very important – *write it down*!

Work with your Partner

Now is the time to start making a plan.

You must *both* agree on what you are going to do and how you are going to go about solving your own problems.

Yes, they are *your* problems and only you can solve them, unless you are about to inherit a fortune or have just won the lottery. But then you would not need my help. So use the Action Point below, and make a start.

You must make sure you both agree with what you are writing down. I have added some ideas of my own, but this is personal to you and *you* must make it work!

ACTION POINT

Take an A4 notepad and write at the top of the front cover:

Action Plan For Wealth

by: [Put your names in here]

We both agree that we have taken our financial future into our hands and we are going to control our finances so we never have to worry again.

and both sign and date it.

Congratulations. You have taken the first step towards recovering your finances, your self-esteem and, most importantly, the knowledge that once your debts have been eradicated your worries will be over for ever!

ACTION POINT

Now you need to sit down with that A4 pad again.

On the next page, divide the page into three columns and write the headings: 'Aims', 'Goals', 'How To Get There'.

Under each heading, write down your aims; not mine, not your bank manager's (although they may converge), but *your* own aims; to get what you want out of this exercise.

Next, write down your goals. Another word for 'goals' is 'dreams'. Write down your dreams and you will make them come true.

Finally, start jotting down notes on how you will achieve your aims and how you will make your dreams come true!

Now you have made a start, review what you have decided to do together. Here, it is important to ensure that you both understand what your aims and goals are and that you share the same aims, goals and agree the actions needed to achieve these.

EXAMPLE

Aims	Goals	How To Get There
Get out of debt	Cut costs	Waste less
		Spend less
		Think before we spend
Start saving	Save regularly	Set up a standing order
Pay off credit cards	Stop using expensive credit cards	Cut up your cards
Reduce outgoings	Move mortgage	Talk to financial advisors

Chapter 2
BUDGETARY CONTROL

Making a budget is the first step to financial independence.

Now is the time to sit down and set your weekly expenditure budget. Yes: weekly, *not* monthly. You will need to start by deciding what the things are upon which you spend money sensibly, and what are frivolous and unnecessary things.

ACTION POINT

Using the work sheet in Chapter 9, (feel free to photocopy this page), please complete to reflect your current spending.

To the right is an example of an expenditure and income sheet. The example shows that after *one* year, Joe Jonas's debt will increase by £5,712.72

If you are in a situation similar to that of Joe Jonas, you have a serious problem. Unless you take control *now*, you will not be able to sustain your lifestyle and may jeopardize your family and your home. So Joe needs to take control of his personal circumstances or he will face certain bankruptcy. If you are in a similar position you *must* review your own expenses and income now and either increase your income or reduce your expenses.

Remember, saving money is putting money back into your pocket.

AN EXAMPLE OF SPENDING MORE THAN YOU EARN: JOE JONAS' SALARY AND EXPENDITURE

Expenses	£
Mortgage/rent	57.59
Council tax	26.92
Electricity	7.23
Water	3.84
Gas	6.51
Credit cards	100.19
Food	39.63
Drink	18.45
Insurance: building/contents	4.44
Insurance: personal/life	2.55
Pension	10.00
Outings, i.e. cinema/theatre	15.25
Eating out	23.78
Holidays	38.46
Papers and magazines	8.29
Motoring expenses	12.45
Petrol	5.40
Christmas and birthdays	25.50
Cash	50.00
Clothes	22.00
Bank interest	27.00
Fixtures, fittings and repairs	
Gambling/Lotto	5.00
Flowers and chocolates	2.50
Wine and alcoholic drinks	12.25
Other	
Total	525.23

Weekly income	£415.38
Weekly expenditure	£525.25
Weekly Deficit (income expenditure)	£109.86
Annual Deficit (weekly deficit * 52)	£5,712.72

Chapter 3

CATEGORISE AND REVIEW YOUR EXPENDITURE

Now is the time to brainstorm and mind map (see Chapter 12) to find out how much you can save and where. First, turn off that TV set! *Eastenders* can wait. Take a close look at your expenses.

ACTION POINT

Using the methods of either mind mapping or brainstorming with your partner/spouse, it is time to see where you can cut down on your outgoings.

Firstly you must define which category best describes your expenses:

- Vital and important
- Important, but can be reduced
- Must be reduced
- Frivolous and must be excluded
- Totally unimportant

As a guide, the following are in the first category of 'vital and important':

- Mortgage/rent
- Council tax
- House insurance
- Credit card payments

The next set are 'important, but can be reduced', they include:

- Heat and light
- Food and drink
- Water
- Credit card payments (see Chapter 8)

The third set, those that must be reduced, include:

- Insurance (personal) and pension
- Papers and magazines
- Motoring expenses (including petrol)
- Clothes
- Holidays
- Christmas and birthday spending
- Cash

And the 'frivolous and must be removed' category may include:

- Chocolates and flowers
- Wine and other alcoholic drinks
- Outings, theatre, cinema, eating out, etc.
- And anything else you spend money on that is neither vital nor important!

The above is an outline and a guide to what you should do and how to go about it. I cannot give you all the answers but a few ideas as to how to cut down your costs are listed below in no particular order:

- Shop around for the cheapest utility suppliers and keep these reviewed; also get an off peak/peak meter for cheaper energy charges.
- Always use the washing machine, tumble dryer, dishwasher and any other random electrical piece of equipment at night when the white meter or economy seven gives you cheaper electricity charges!
- Always turn out the lights when you are not in a room, it is amazing how much electricity a light bulb uses (and you will be doing the environment a favour).
- Turn off the radios and TVs and computers that are left on standby, as this costs money without you knowing it.
- Turn the thermostat down by five degrees; you will reduce your heating bills drastically and you will still be warm. Do the same for your hot water.

- In the colder months, keep doors and windows closed, especially internal doors, to retain heat and keep heating costs down.

- Wear thicker clothes and sweaters inside in winter.

- When boiling a kettle for a cup of tea or coffee, only boil enough for your requirements. Do not boil enough to feed an army!

- Walk to the shops (if you can) to reduce your expenditure on petrol, and reduce pollution at the same time.

- Use public transport wherever possible, car-share or even walk; petrol and car park charges are extremely expensive.

- Newspapers cost on average five pounds a week (that's £260 a year) and few of us read a paper properly, cover to cover. So listen to or watch the news on your radio or TV. Libraries carry newspapers; there may be papers provided at your place of work; you may be able to look at a friend's. However, do not read them in a shop.

- Use second class post; there is little difference in the extra day that second class takes!

- When you drive, go a few miles per hour slower and drive smoothly: do not floor the accelerator or your fuel consumption will rocket!

- Like Barbara and Tom Good of *The Good Life*, grow your own food. It is surprising how much you can grow in a small bed. Salads grow well in a flower border. Tomatoes flourish on a patio or even window box. Herbs also grow well in pots. Even carrots, courgettes and beans are easy to grow and help you to save substantially on your grocery bills.

- Take your own drinks and packed lunches/sandwiches to work, it is amazing how much a drink and a sandwich cost to buy compared with making your own!

- If you like to have a drink in the evening, have a pint of water first, it cuts down on the amount of alcohol your stomach can hold and reduces your 'Wine and alcoholic drinks' cost, or cut them out altogether (even if it is just in the week).

- If you use a mobile phone, use pre-pay to reduce the costs.
- Make your home efficient: use draft proofing, insulation, double glazing and other efficiency measures to reduce heat loss from your home. Look into installing solar panels to save on electricity costs. Local Authority grants may be available to help you here.

Brainstorming with your partner with a large, blank sheet of paper will help you work out precisely what you can reduce on your expenditure list, and remember: have fun. This is serious and needs to be taken seriously, but if you take it too seriously it will become a chore. Think of it as an adventure on which you are both embarking.

If you like the idea of mind mapping, see my examples and ideas in Chapter 12 and, by all means, mind map as a way of reaching the best answers for you.

Debt is debt. It is what you owe and you must take responsibility for it. You cannot make it less by giving it to someone else to look after unless it really costs you less.

Chapter 4

ASSETS, LIABILITIES AND DEBT CONSOLIDATION

You may have seen the numerous and tedious adverts in the press, on TV and even posted through your door telling you that you can consolidate your debt (usually as a home owner) at a terrific, low rate of interest.

Let's say you receive a leaflet through your letter box from Company A. They want to consolidate your debts at their current interest rates of 12.7% with a small print clause that there would also be a fee of up to 10% of the amount borrowed.

Thus, over five years (ignoring the fact that they reserve the rights to raise their rates of interest), the real cost of borrowing was actually 14.7%.

Terrific? *No*. Terrifying? Yes.

Bank base rate	4.75%
Card base rate	12.7%
Extra fee	10%
Actual rate over five years	14.75%
Loan	20,000

ASSETS, LIABILITIES AND DEBT CONSOLIDATION

	Existing loan (£20,000)	New loan	Difference[1]
Owed to credit card company	Monthly interest, debt and mortgage	Monthly interest	
over one month	£384.33	£521.08	£136.75
over one year	£4,612	£6,253	£1,641
over five years	£23,055	£21,360	£8,205
over ten years	£46,199	£62,529	£16,410

With bank base rates at 4.75%, that means they are charging 10% over base.

Let's take an example: on a debt of £20,000, you would pay £521.08 a month over a five-year period (a total of £31,265.86 over the period). Over ten years that would cost you £351.57 a month (a total of £42,188.52 over the period). If you added the debt of £20,000 on to your mortgage it would cost you £384.33 a month over five years (a total of 23,059.80 over the period) and £219.53 over ten year (a total of £26,340 over the period); a saving of £8,206.06 over five years and £15,848.52 over ten years compared with the expensive credit card offer!

So is debt consolidation a good idea?

My calculations show that you are being sucked even deeper into the quagmire of debt by using bad forms of debt consolidation

---

[1] Notes on calculation:

The calculations in column one, Existing Loan (£20,000) is the effect of adding the credit card debt of £20,000 to your mortgage over a short five to ten year period.

The calculation in the second column is the new consolidated loan with Company A at their rates of 12.7 (grossed up to include their charges) over a five to ten year period.

In the third column we have the difference or the extra cost the advertising company would charge vs. your own mortgage company (building society or bank) showing the savings over one month, one year, five years and tens years.

Here we can see that the attractive 'New Loan' is more like that from a loan shark and is highly expensive with punitive tie-ins such as early repayment penalties. Your building society is much more likely the better provider in this case.

However there are credit card companies that offer balance transfers with an initial period of zero per cent interest, so for those who want to shop around (see the website recommendations in Appendix 1: Useful Contacts) there are some good deals available… but beware!

ACTION POINT

Check your credit card interest rate *now* and use the internet to compare what you might be able to get.[2] If you succeed in getting a better deal and saving yourself money, reward yourself with a nice bottle of wine, a box of chocolates or by taking the family to the cinema!

Change for change's sake is bad. Change for your improvement is good.

---

[2] Try www.moneyexpert.co.uk.

Chapter 5
SMALL AND SUBTLE CHANGES

Change can be a frightening course to take but it can, and often does, lead to great improvements. So when viewing changes, grasp those changes with a steady hand and look at them in the full knowledge that it is *you* who will be better off and you will be thankful you made those changes that so improved your life.

By making small, subtle lifestyle changes, you will make large savings.

You could:

- Use a telephone system that is free to those people you call (TelecomPlus amongst others offer this – this means calls to friends and family can cost you nothing!)

- Use mobile pre-pay cards.

- Make your telephone calls after six o'clock at night.

- In colder weather wear a thicker sweater rather than turn the heating up. Close windows and doors to conserve heat.

- Turn out the lights when you leave a room.

By adopting these small habits, you will find that although your actual lifestyle will alter only very slightly, your household expenses will plummet. Adopting healthy habits will not only improve your finances but will improve your feel-good factor considerably.

These little lifestyle changes are the most important and vital part of this whole exercise. Go in with a positive mental attitude and you will come out a winner. Let's recap on the lessons you have learned so far:

- Do not believe the adverts that urge you to 'consolidate your debt'; this could cause you more pain than you may imagine.

- By talking to and trusting your spouse/partner, you will work together to solve this and other problems as they occur.
- Do not waste money on things that you do not need.
- Stay clear of credit card companies and loan sharks who will charge you high interest rates.

In summary:

- Cut your costs to a level that helps you keep within your budget. You will then save money.
- Be sensible: put on thicker clothes before you decide to turn up the heating. Close doors, windows and curtains to keep in heat.
- Don't consolidate your loans unless the interest rates are cheaper and the time scales are the same as the loans you already have.
- Don't ever fall into the spend-yourself-out-of-trouble trap, it puts you in deeper.
- Do reward yourself and congratulate yourself on your own success when you finally achieve independence.
- Do take care when shopping; shopping for foods that you can prepare will always be better value than ready meals.
- When out shopping and something catches your eye and you think 'I must have that!'

  STOP.
  WAIT.
  THINK.

  Ask yourself:
  - Do I need it now? No.
  - Do I want it? Yes.
  - Can I afford it? No.
  - Can I wait? Yes.

  If you answered yes to the last question, wait, and then ask yourself the same questions in four weeks' time; the chances are that you will not want to buy it. If you take control, you will win.

Chapter 6
WHAT DO YOU WANT?

This may be the toughest question posed by this book. If you do not answer it, you will be like a boat without a rudder, drifting on an ocean without direction.

ACTION POINT

You need to take up your notepad again and write down the following headings, leaving a page for each and writing the subheadings on each page with four or five lines between each.

1. Where am I now? (work/home/family/possessions/debt)
2. Where do I want to be? (same subheadings)
3. What do I need to do get there?
4. What do I need others (specify whom) to do to help me get there?
5. What time scale am I going to allow? (Be realistic. For example, two months to start things off and twelve months to achieve main aims.)

Bear in mind that your circumstances and your goals will be personal to you and your partner. You will need to answer these questions together. Turn that telly off. This will become the map that will help you find your way through the financial minefields of life.

This will be the foundation on which your future financial well-being is based; if you do not build sound foundations, your financial future will crumble and rot. So be very careful and patient; you don't want your finances crashing down around your ears.

Build your foundations with titanium, steel and reinforced concrete. Live it, believe it and you will succeed. This really will be the best investment you ever made.

Write it down! This is a tip I learned early in my career. Keep a record of everything you spend. Yes, *everything*.

Once you have a week's record of what you spend your money on, you will be able to set the items on which you spend in the margin of a weekly spend diary.

From here, you will be able to define clearly from what and where savings can be made! It may be those cappuccinos, it may be newspapers and magazines. It may be the pub or those expensive sandwiches from the rip-off sandwich bar. I don't know, but an expenses book will show you where you can save serious money on a weekly basis!

Chapter 7
THE NITTY GRITTY

Spend little; save a lot!

Now, if you followed chapter five to the letter, you will know where you are going and how you are going to get there.

Number one rule may be to 'downsize', but do not see this as a backward step. It is the first step in rebuilding your financial world and even though you may view it as a backwards move, it is actually the reverse; it may be the impetus that actually takes you forward faster than anything else.

'Downsize?' I hear you say. 'What? Sell up? Move?'

So ask yourself, and your local estate agent, 'How much is my house worth? How much is it really worth on the market if I want to sell without a problem?'

Take the amount you still need to repay on your mortgage and deduct this from your sale price after costs (i.e. solicitor and estate agent) and you will have the equity you own in your own home:

Sale price	£310,000
Mortgage	£65,000
Costs	£6,300
Equity	£238,700

In this case could you buy a house for £250,000 with a tiny mortgage and save yourself about £275 a month.

ACTION POINT

You will need to do some research: can you buy a house in the area where you can happily live for £250,000? If not, then can you move to an area that will enable you to buy a home for £250,000 and not spend a fortune on travelling to work?

Remember, here we are talking short term, one to five years, enough time to rebuild your finances and have a financial future with a sound footing. Enough time to build up your savings. Enough time to get back on your feet financially. Then you can look into buying a larger home, if you need one, in the future. But only when you have your foundations totally secure. You do not want to slip back into debt. Do not fall into the 'keeping up with the Joneses' trap. People often think, or say, a variety of things when they are faced with downsizing. These include:

- We need enough rooms in case our parents/children want to come and stay (but how often does that happen in reality?)
- We need room for friends.
- We need rooms for grandchildren.
- What would our friends and relatives think?
- I could not possibly have a house with only two bedrooms!

Well, one couple I know bought a large five bedroom house so that their children and parents could come and stay. The only trouble was that the parents came once a year for one night (or two) at Christmas time and the children had a bedroom of their own which remained empty for more than ten months of the year.

Finally they saw that the debt they were getting into by having such a costly home to run was immense and that in fact they were working for the bank manager and/or building society. They sold their house and downsized to a home with three bedrooms (still two bedrooms for guests). The equity they had in the house they sold enabled them to buy a nice home with only a small mortgage and created a huge improvement in their lifestyle – and no more debts!

They are now saving and will very soon be able to buy a second home for holidays or retirement. I have attached a copy of their budget before and after the move below.

CURRENT BUDGET, FUTURE BUDGET

Expenses	Now	Future
Mortgage/rent	57.59	12.50
Council tax	26.92	16.23
Electricity	7.23	4.55
Water	3.84	2.55
Gas	6.51	4.43
Credit cards	100.19	0
Food	39.63	40
Drink	18.45	14
Insurance: building/contents	4.44	3.50
Insurance: personal/life	2.55	2.55
Pension	10.00	10.00
Outings, i.e. cinema/theatre	15.25	15.25
Eating out	23.78	10.00
Holidays	38.46	12.00
Papers and magazines	8.29	0
Motoring expenses	12.45	7.5
Petrol	5.40	3.00
Christmas and birthdays	25.50	12.00
Cash	50.00	8.00
Clothes	22.00	5.00
Bank interest	27.00	0
Fixtures, fittings and repairs		0
Gambling/Lotto	5.00	0
Flowers and chocolates	2.50	0
Wine and alcoholic drinks	12.25	0
Other		
Total	525.23	188.06
Weekly savings		337.19

In our example, Mr and Mrs Five Beds saved themselves £17,534 a year. That amounts to £87,670 over five years. Putting those savings into a deposit account would enable Mr and Mrs Five Beds to move to a larger house, or just have a really comfortable nest egg… and no more debt!

'No way,' you say. 'I like it here, I am comfortable.'

Well, stop. Let's take another look. Go to your budget sheet. How much is your mortgage costing you each month? Could you reduce your mortgage and buy a house that has sufficient space for you but at a lesser cost? If so, what is stopping you? And if selling and moving is not an option, how about considering letting a room or two to a lodger? It could be a young professional, a student or a friend. Or you could even run a small bed and breakfast concern. The choices may be limitless! (Please remember, though, that if you are running a business you may need to talk to your accountant about the tax implications.)

Chapter 8
CREDIT CARDS AND SECURITY

Look very carefully at your monthly spend on your credit cards. You may be in a similar position to a colleague of mine who racks up debts of £20,000 or £30,000 and lives close to, or at the limit of his credit. What is worse is that they are only paying off very little of the original debt, so the interest they are paying is massive.

Take control. Firstly agree as to whether you will keep the cards – some of them or none at all. Then make a repayment plan to reduce the excessive costs you are incurring. Next, look to move the debt to a credit card that charges you no or little interest on the transferred balance. Do not keep paying the penal level of interest that most cards charge. Perhaps you should look at keeping only the cards that are charge cards. These cards are paid off every month, so there is no monthly minimum – just what you owe and therefore no costly interest!

Watch out for credit card and bank statement fraud. Today it appears to be easier to earn a living by using someone else's credit cards or bank account than working for a living. It is not only easier, but it is also illegal and immoral. The trouble is that most people are careless with their identity. They throw bank statements into the dustbin for others to find. They bawl their credit card number down the telephone, oblivious to any one listening. They discard council tax bills, credit card slips, letters and building society account/mortgage account information so others can find it. Suddenly somebody else can 'become' you and either use your credit rating to buy things, get a mobile phone (or worse), use your bank account and credit cards.

'So what?' you ask. 'It won't happen to me.' Well, my friends, here you are wrong. When living in Surrey, my wife and I found that someone who we did not know had attempted to take £12,000 from our building society account.

On a separate occasion when we sold our house, the new owner used letters that were not forwarded by the Post Office to get credit to buy a car – defaulted – and our credit score was compromised. Now we shred everything.

I recommend that everyone buy a shredder. You should shred all paperwork that has your name and address on it. There have been reports of clever people using video cameras to spy on ATM machines and actually track people using these to steal their numbers, pick pocket their wallets and use their money.

Question: How long does it take to get money from an ATM?
Answer: Less than two minutes.

Question: How many minutes to use three or four ATMs to raid your accounts?
Answer: Ten minutes.

Two or ten minutes to make you significantly worse off. And how many shops can be visited in the next ten minutes using up your valuable spare available credit on your credit card?

- Do I cut up my credit cards?
- Do I act responsibly and protect my credit cards?
- Or do I act as a careful prudent person in the way I spend with my cards?

The choice is yours alone!

Tip
Keep your credit card receipts and at the end of each month when you get your credit card statement, carefully check your bills. Do the same with your bank account each month. In short, trust no one but yourselves and never trust your bank or credit card company to look after you!

A Cash-Spend Lifestyle

Perhaps you would prefer to control your saving by drawing a set sum every week and once you have spent that sum – well, there is nothing left until next week.

So set your weekly target (excluding the direct debit bills), say £200, and once you have spent that £200, there is nothing left, so you cannot spend anything else until next Monday. Rethink your costs; rethink your lifestyle.

Chapter 9
REDRAW YOUR BUDGETS

From here on it is all down to you.

ACTION POINT

You should use the budgetary control sheet in this chapter (copy as many as you feel necessary) to assess your weekly expenditure.

Well, now comes the really hard part: using the knowledge and tips you have gathered so far, you must work out what your new budget will look like.

To make life a little easier, I have attached four copies to this chapter so you can work through it *now* using these pages as work sheets – and I would recommend using pencil and rubber. Look at your current costs and see by how much you can reduce these.

I would urge you to complete this chapter and then reward yourself with whatever takes your fancy: a chocolate, a cake, a pint, whatever you really like. You deserve it. You have done well so far.

But this is only the starting point!

Expenses	Now	Future
Mortgage/rent		
Council tax		
Electricity		
Water		
Gas		
Credit cards		
Food		
Insurance: building/contents		
Insurance: personal/life		
Pension		
Outings, i.e. cinema/theatre		
Eating out		
Holidays		
Papers and magazines		
Motoring expenses		
Petrol		
Christmas and birthdays		
Cash		
Clothes		
Bank interest		
Fixtures, fittings and repairs		
Gambling/Lotto		
Flowers and chocolates		
Wine and alcoholic drinks		
Other		
Total		
Weekly savings		

Expenses	Now	Future
Mortgage/rent		
Council tax		
Electricity		
Water		
Gas		
Credit cards		
Food		
Insurance: building/contents		
Insurance: personal/life		
Pension		
Outings, i.e. cinema/theatre		
Eating out		
Holidays		
Papers and magazines		
Motoring expenses		
Petrol		
Christmas and birthdays		
Cash		
Clothes		
Bank interest		
Fixtures, fittings and repairs		
Gambling/Lotto		
Flowers and chocolates		
Wine and alcoholic drinks		
Other		
Total		
Weekly savings		

Expenses	Now	Future
Mortgage/rent		
Council tax		
Electricity		
Water		
Gas		
Credit cards		
Food		
Insurance: building/contents		
Insurance: personal/life		
Pension		
Outings, i.e. cinema/theatre		
Eating out		
Holidays		
Papers and magazines		
Motoring expenses		
Petrol		
Christmas and birthdays		
Cash		
Clothes		
Bank interest		
Fixtures, fittings and repairs		
Gambling/Lotto		
Flowers and chocolates		
Wine and alcoholic drinks		
Other		
Total		
Weekly savings		

Expenses	Now	Future
Mortgage/rent		
Council tax		
Electricity		
Water		
Gas		
Credit cards		
Food		
Insurance: building/contents		
Insurance: personal/life		
Pension		
Outings, i.e. cinema/theatre		
Eating out		
Holidays		
Papers and magazines		
Motoring expenses		
Petrol		
Christmas and birthdays		
Cash		
Clothes		
Bank interest		
Fixtures, fittings and repairs		
Gambling/Lotto		
Flowers and chocolates		
Wine and alcoholic drinks		
Other		
Total		
Weekly savings		

Chapter 10
SEEK PROFESSIONAL ADVICE

Seek advice but watch your costs.

This is a vital part of any ongoing financial planning. It is a common misconception that financial advice is expensive or will cost you money. With a little research and investigation you will find that you can get a huge amount of financial advice, and very good and worthwhile financial advice, for virtually nothing.

Use the telephone to find people who will give you advice or, at the very least, an initial consultation for free. The first person to call is an independent financial advisor (you can find out where to find one of these in the back of this book). Secondly, contact any or all from the list below:

- Bank manager
- Debt counsellor
- Citizens Advice Bureau
- Accountant
- Credit card company
- Financial advisor
- Solicitor
- Building society staff
- Mortgage advisor

Before you go along to any consultation ensure that there are no charges and then send the advisor a list of your assets, liabilities, your income statements and your current budget. Also ask them if they want anything else and prepare a list of questions and items you wish to discuss with them. The better prepared you are, the more you will gain from the meeting and the better the outcome will be.

Note
The 'Seven Ps' principle is a valuable tool to remember:

Proper

Prior

Preparation

Prevents

Piss

Poor

Performance

If you can, set out a budget of current expenses and a proposed budget for their consideration. Use one of the pro formas in Chapter 9 to set out your current budget and your ideas of reducing your outgoings as noted above.

Specimen Questions

- I need to get my expenses below my income level: how can I do this?
- I want to start saving money *now*! Where can I reduce my outgoings and expenses?
- Who is the cheapest...
  ...credit card company?
  ...loan provider?
  ...life insurance company?
  ...supermarket? (i.e. Asda, Tesco, Morrisons, Waitrose, etc.)
  ...petrol station?

The Cost of your Lifestyle: Your Mortgage

This is usually the largest part of any household's outgoings and is therefore a critical part of the way we look at our outgoings.

Here are some questions you may want to ask yourself:

- Do I really want to live in such an expensive area?
- Do I need such a large house with such a large mortgage?
- Can I live in the same size house at a cheaper cost, maintain my quality of life and still get to work?
- Can I get the same mortgage for a lower monthly cost?
- Can I sell my house and buy a smaller house and have no mortgage at all?
- Can I get as good a job as I currently have in a less expensive housing area?

Should you decide to sell up and buy a new house, then you must research which estate agent will offer you the best commission rate and yet still sell your property quickly.

Remember, you must buy what you need at the lowest prices possible! To do that, you need to continuously watch for who is charging how much. With petrol, this is relatively easy, as petrol stations have their prices advertised prominently. For food and drink you have to shop around, but beware of running up a petrol bill of £1 to save 10p!

With utility bills you need to go to the supplier who will guarantee you the lowest gas and electricity prices in the UK.

Other questions to address are:

- Do I need such a large/expensive/thirsty car?
- Can I get the rate I pay on hire purchase down without huge penalties?
- Do we need two cars?
- Do we need two cars and a motorbike?
- Could we walk our children to school?
- Could we walk to the shops?
- Can I walk, cycle or catch public transport to work?
- Can I car-share?

If you are considering moving you should ask yourself if the area you are moving to has:

- a good level of public transport;
- a post bus – a rural speciality!
- a reasonable level of council tax;
- good schools close by;
- sustainable job opportunities;
- good future development plans;
- up-to-date infrastructure; and
- good future infrastructure plans.

Chapter 11
MY JOB

This is rather a dramatic chapter as it asks some really hard questions that need very careful consideration.

Try these to start:

- Does my job pay the best going rate I can get?
- Can I get better pay from the same job with a different employer?
- If I move, can I get the same job in the new area I want to move to paying the same or better money?
- Can I do a job that I would find more interesting, challenging, exciting, fun and enjoyable?
- What other job can I do/do I want to do/would suit my lifestyle?

Why ask these questions?

I once met a guy who had worked for the same company for twenty years. In chatting to him, I said that he must really love his job to have stayed twenty years.

'No,' he replied. 'I hate it. It's the most boring job in the world and my boss is an arse.'

I was puzzled and asked him why he stayed instead of leaving to get a job he loved.

His response astounded me.

He said, 'When I reach the age of sixty-five and retire, I get a great pension; then I can really start to enjoy myself.'

He was crackers. He would have spent over forty-five years, the best years of his life, working in a job he hated so he could retire at sixty-five with a good pension. And who knows how much longer he had to live!

My heartfelt advice for everyone is: enjoy doing your job or leave and get a job you enjoy! You never know when you might die or how fit you will be when you retire. You may die aged fifty-two or sixty-seven or eighty-six or ninety-one but when you die, please ensure that you have enjoyed *all* of your life!

But stop. Don't just hand in your notice!

- Look into who is hiring staff now.
- Look at the job rate of pay. Is it right?
- Do you have what they are looking for, or can you show them that you have?

Different Jobs

First, look at what you are doing now. Do you like your job? Make a list of those things that:

- you would like to do.
- you would hate to do.

Then if you change jobs, can you find a job that:

- you can do?
- you would enjoy?
- pays as well or better?
- is more fun?

Complete the following:

What do you enjoy about your job?

_____
_____
_____
_____

What do you dislike about your job?

_____
_____
_____
_____

Now, using the job sheet below, start to think about what job sector you may wish to be in (this list is far from exhaustive).

- Sales
- Shop/Retail
- Office (admin, secretarial)
- Office (management)
- Janitorial
- Security
- Manual
- Mechanical/engineering
- Semi-skilled
- Skilled
- Architectural/surveying
- Financial services
- Call centre/Telesales
- Hotel/Catering
- Human Resources
- Banking
- Insurance
- Gardening
- Contracting
- Farming
- Veterinary
- Gardening/Horticulture
- Media (Press/Radio/TV/Films)
- Legal
- Manufacturing
- Education
- Local Government
- Civil Service

Career Changes

So, who can you talk to about a career change?

Well, apart from talking to professional career advisors and the Citizens Advice Bureau, you can chat to your friends. Let them know that you may be in the market for not only a job but a career change, and that you want to know more about every job that might suit you. It is amazing that people will talk for hours about what they like and don't about their jobs. With a little detective work you will be able to discover many jobs that might suit you.

Once you have these (and do write a brief synopsis of each job down), be selective and really assess which really would suit you.

On a piece of paper do the 'Churchill Close'. See the form below:

Job – Pros	Job – Cons

Now you can work out which jobs might suit you and which might not. You may even be lucky enough to find a potential employer who will allow you work experience (for free), or you may be able to 'ghost' a friend at work, i.e. follow and see what he or she does, helping him or her where appropriate.

Remember, the more detective work you do on your potential new job, the better armed you will be when it comes to interviews. I remember once hearing of a guy who applied for a job with Mitchell and Butlers brewery in Birmingham. When asked why he wanted to work for them, he replied that he liked the taste of their mild beer. Of course, he did not get the job!

'Be prepared' is a really good motto!

CHAPTER 12
SPECIAL TOOLS TO HELP YOU

Mind Mapping

The creation of Tony Buzan in the early 1970s, mind mapping is a good system to help you plan.

The advantage of using tools such as mind mapping is that they give you easier access to your brain's full potential. Mind mapping helps activate the whole brain, it lets you develop a logical sequence and detailed organisation of your affairs – in this case, your financial affairs. It also encourages spontaneity and imagination and lets you represent a massive amount of information in a relatively small space.

Using different colours and symbols for different elements of your expenditure and budget will help you identify the essentials from the frivolous and the necessary from the wasteful elements of your daily spend. Mind mapping can let you see the whole picture in overview and detail and is fun.

Use colours, pictures and symbols as well as words.

Lateral Thinking[3]

Use lateral thinking powers to help you see the problem from a different angle. Not everything is black and white, there are many different ways to view a problems. The difference between vertical and lateral thinking is that vertical thinking is sequential whereas lateral thinking allows you to 'jump' from idea to solution.

---

[3] See Edward De Bono, *Lateral Thinking: A Textbook of Creativity*, London, Penguin, 1990.

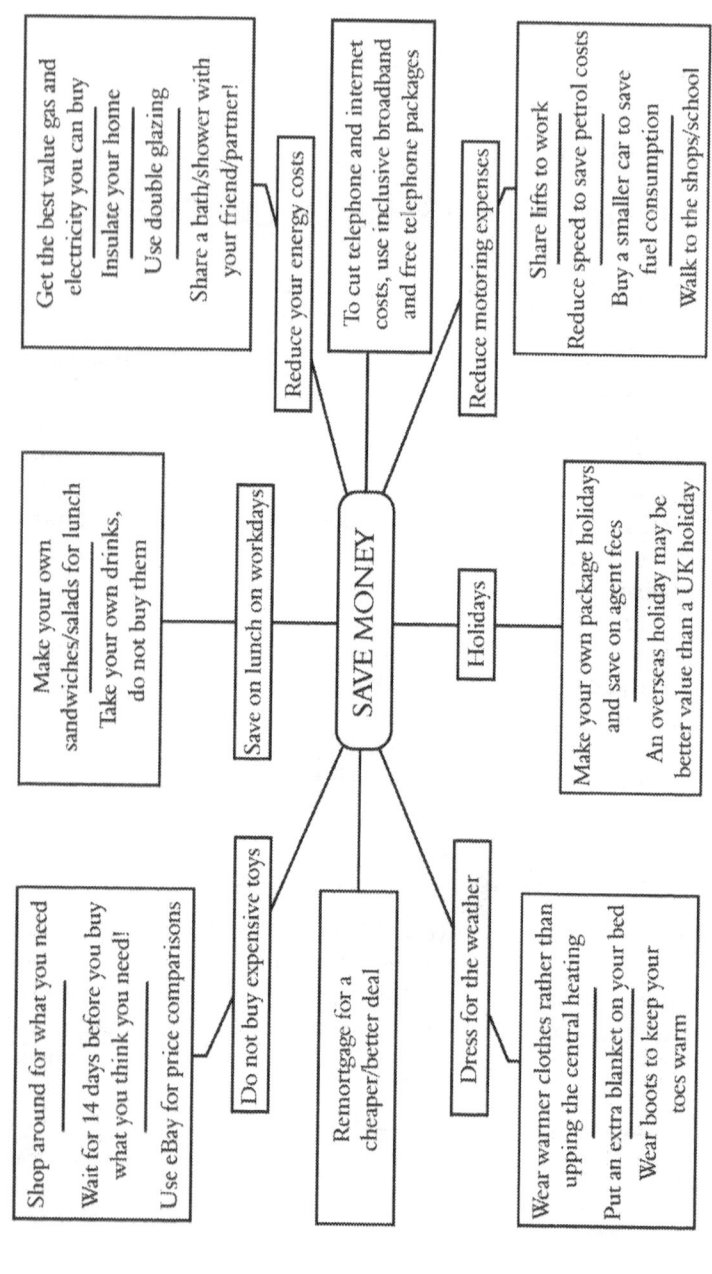

SPECIAL TOOLS TO HELP YOU

Look at this example:

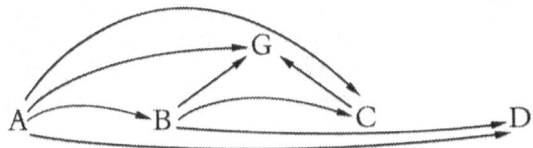

You can jump from any of A, B, C or D to G, without going through A to D. This allows you to look at the least likely paths, as well as the most likely, to solve your problem. Lateral thinking is a creative way of looking at problems that may not necessary need a logical view to achieve a desired outcome.

For example, take this picture of a boy on a park bench. Describe it as follows:

- Lazy boy doing nothing;
- Still room left for others to sit next to boy on bench;
- Boy keeping area of bench dry.

Play It Forward

The entire function of this book is to get you to help yourself. However, unless we all take responsibility for helping others as well as ourselves, we are disassociating ourselves from the human race and this is wrong.

We have a moral and social obligation to help our fellows. One way to do this is to introduce my book and ethics to others so they may climb out of the desperate pit of financial instability and escape the suffering it brings, or at least avoid the pitfalls and build a culture of savings around their own world.

You will also be helping a poor, struggling writer to achieve greater recognition.

It is amazing that by 'playing it forward' you find that things happen to you: nice things, surprising things, things that make you wonder and realise what a joy it is to be a part of the caring human race.

Chapter 13
AVOID BANKRUPTCY

If you avoid bankruptcy there are many advantages for you:
- You avoid the fear of losing your home.
- Your employer need not know about your financial situation.
- If you are in business you will be able to continue to trade.
- You may still be able to obtain credit.
- Creditors will stop harassing you.
- You remain in control of your financial affairs.
- You avoid interviews with 'officialdom'.
- You avoid inspection by outsiders of your personal records.

How can this be achieved? Each person's situation is, of course, different and the circumstances of each will determine what can be done and what may be appropriate. Some steps to take might be:
- debt reduction and arbitration;
- negotiation and early settlement;
- informal voluntary arrangements;
- mortgage/remortgage;
- liaison with 'aggressive' creditors;
- review and repair of credit references; and
- clearing county court judgements.

Surviving Bankruptcy

Mr Morgan[4] was a trader with his own business. His wife had her own design business. They had two children of school age and

---

[4] Note: certain names and details have been changed to protect the privacy of the persons involved.

owned a large house in a desirable area that had a mortgage outstanding. Mr Morgan's business was becoming insolvent but Mrs Morgan had no problems. Mr Morgan wanted to know what to do to safeguard his position and was concerned that he might lose the family home.

Mr Morgan had no savings from his business and his only significant asset was his interest in the matrimonial home. As there was little prospect of him being able to obtain regular work if his business shut down and because Mr Morgan did not want to have sell the family home to raise some cash, a voluntary arrangement was not appropriate. This left the option of trying to struggle on or to await bankruptcy.

After a review we found that Mrs Morgan had been married before and had contributed her divorce settlement monies to the purchase of the family home. It was Mr Morgan's first marriage. In addition a number of improvements and building works had been carried out. The family home was worth £375,000 with equity, after deducting the mortgage of £200,000.

We advised Mr Morgan to petition for his own bankruptcy which would immediately remove all the pressure and stress of creditors pressing for payment, whilst enabling Mr Morgan to concentrate on protecting the family home from any claim the trustee in bankruptcy might make.

A trustee was appointed and, as we expected, he immediately claimed that he was entitled to half of the equity, i.e. £100,000. We then advised Mrs Morgan to lodge a claim with the trustee saying that she was entitled to the £150,000 from the equity, that being the sum which had been put into the property as a deposit from her divorce and that she had never gifted any of that money to Mr Morgan. The trustee had to accept, but then asked £25,000, being half the balance after deducting £150,000. We then advised Mrs Morgan to tell the trustee that she had paid for the costs of building works and improvements to the property and to provide copies of bills, etc. to support the claim. As Mr Morgan had earned little or no money in the period, it was clear that Mrs Morgan would have had to pay for these works.

Ultimately, the trustee agreed to accept £5,000 for Mr Morgan's interest in the property, instead of the £100,000, which appeared at first to be available.

COMMENT

Because Mr and Mrs Morgan took advice, they were able to protect the family home. Without assistance from experienced insolvency personnel, the Morgans could easily have accepted the trustee's claim at face value and either had to increase their mortgage or sell the home to raise the £100,000 asked for. Thus a careful review of circumstances can reveal information that may assist in the protection of assets.

Voluntary Arrangement

Mrs Blythe[5] had a business which, because of financial difficulties, had to cease trading. She had no other assets than the monies that were due to her business and items owned by the business. Mrs Blythe could not be certain of her future income but knew that there was not enough money to pay off her creditors in full.

When we spoke to Mrs Blythe we looked at the assets of the business. There were certainly monies to come in, but insufficient to meet the debts. Having looked at what would be available to creditors if Mrs Blythe became bankrupt, it was considered that the return to the creditors in a voluntary arrangement would be better if the costs were kept to a minimum.

Mrs Blythe was anxious to avoid bankruptcy and on this basis asked an insolvency practitioner to assist in negotiating and drafting a voluntary arrangement proposal simply on the basis that the return to creditors would be better than in bankruptcy.

The voluntary arrangement proposal was approved.

COMMENT

Whilst most voluntary arrangements require some form of regular contribution, in this instance, even where there were no contributions, the insolvency practitioner and Mrs Blythe were able to demonstrate that the return would be better than in bankruptcy, and so the creditors accepted a voluntary arrangement and Mrs Blythe was saved from bankruptcy.

---

[5] Note: certain names and details have been changed to protect the privacy of the persons involved.

The Truth About Bankruptcy

Bankruptcy must not be taken lightly. It should not be considered if you have assets of any reasonable value and you own your own home, jointly or personally (unlike Mr Morgan whose home was owned by Mrs Morgan) even if there is little or no equity. Contrary to what might be said about the new Enterprise Act – which states that certain classifications of bankrupts could be discharged in twelve months – this will happen in relatively few cases, and it should be remembered that the stigma of bankruptcy will probably *never* go away.

Even after being discharged, it can affect your ability to obtain a mortgage or get credit for many years to come. Being declared bankrupt is a very public matter. Some of the effects are:

- Bankruptcy is always advertised; the bankruptcy application will be advertised in the London Gazette and the local press where you live.

- Notification is made to everyone financially connected; your bank, building society, creditors, landlord, etc. will be informed immediately.

- Bankrupts cannot run a business; any business you own will be closed immediately.

- Any asset that might have been acquired during the term of the bankruptcy – including inheritances, insurance pay-outs/maturities, equity in property, windfalls, and possibly pension income – will be lost.

- Bank accounts and credit cards will be closed. Anything that is being purchased by lease or HP, such as your car, will be immediately returned to its owner.

- People that have been bankrupt previously should be very careful about being made bankrupt again, as the minimum period of bankruptcy is five years, and could continue for up to fifteen years before being discharged.

- Certain employment situations will be prejudiced by being declared bankrupt, and professional and business status will be lost. Membership of many associations and societies will also be lost.

The Myths

'They will not take my house, it is in negative equity.'

The Official Receiver will place a charge on the property, effectively preventing its sale and will wait, long after your bankruptcy has been discharged, to get his hands on any available equity that has come about due to increased property values.

'They won't take my home, I am married with a young family.'

They will, unless your partner can prove that he or she has an interest in the property, in which case the Official Receiver will allow your partner to purchase your share of the equity. If they are unable to do this, then the trustee in bankruptcy will, after twelve months, have the right to obtain possession and subsequently issue an eviction order.

'I put my home into my partner's name years ago.'

They will take your home, unless you can prove that your partner paid the full value at the time of the transfer and has since paid the mortgage in full. You will also have to account for the funds.

'My new business is in my partner's name, and all profits will be taken by my partner.'

This is regarded as a criminal activity by the trustees in bankruptcy and any assets earned during the bankruptcy will be forfeit.

Chapter 14
BE A WINNER

Be a winner, not a loser. This is really a state of mind.

- A winner makes mistakes and says 'OK, so I was wrong', and learns from his mistakes. A loser says 'It wasn't my fault.'
- A winner credits his good luck when he wins, even though it was not luck; a loser credits his bad luck for losing, even though it was not luck.
- A winner works harder than a loser and yet has more time. A loser is always too busy; *too busy* staying a failure.
- A winner works through problems; a loser goes around problems.
- A winner says sorry by making up for it; a loser says he's sorry, but makes the same mistakes over and over.
- A winner knows what to fight for and what to compromise on. A loser compromises on what he should fight for and fights when he should compromise.
- A winner says, 'I am good but not as good as I could be or ought to be.' A loser says, 'I'm not as bad as a lot of people.' A winner looks up to where he is going; a loser looks down on people who have yet to achieve the position he is in.
- A winner respects those superior to him and tries to learn from them; a loser resents those superior to him and finds fault.
- A winner is responsible for more than just his job; a loser says, 'I only work here!'
- A winner says, 'There ought to be a better way of doing this'; a loser says, 'Why change it? That's the way it's always been done.'

Chapter 15
SUMMARY

If by using my ideology and methods you are able to reduce your outgoings and increase your savings then I have succeeded, as have you!

Well done.

If I have given you just a spark of how to avoid financial disasters then that is great!

If you enjoyed working with me on solving your own problems, then congratulations. But remember others may also need my help and you can help them by example (or by buying them my book as a present).

My sole aim is to stop people being dragged into the quagmire of debt that is primarily caused by the credit card companies and banks offering credit, loans and money to everyone and anyone without first getting the borrower to really analyse his or her financial situation.

Many people are egged on to buy that new car on low finance when:

- there is nothing wrong with their old one;
- they will be losing thousands of pounds in depreciation;
- they really cannot afford to buy the new one; and
- if it were not for the pressures from their peers, the press and the government-driven material society in which we live, then the new car would remain in the car showroom where it belongs until a new car is a necessity, not a luxury.

The same is true of many purchases, from stereos to computers; from mobile phones to ipods; from TVs to 'toys for the boys' style gadgets; from carpets to new dining tables.

So be circumspect. Ask yourself, before buying, 'Do I need this?' And then instead of buying immediately, *wait*!

Wait for two weeks and then see if you really want it, see if you can really afford it, and if both answers are yes, then maybe you should go ahead.

In the end, it's all up to you. I can only offer guidance and ideas; you have to put these into action, so good luck.

Remember to use the work sheets and fill in the gaps. Make this your book but, most of all, have *fun*: if you don't make this fun, it won't work.

Appendix 1
USEFUL CONTACTS

Citizens Advice Bureau	www.citizensadvice.org.uk	0870 126 4010
The Personal Finance Society	www.thepfs.org	020 8530 0852
IFA Promotion	www.unbiased.co.uk	0800 085 3250
FSA	www.fsa.gov.uk	
Financial Ombudsman	http://www.financial-ombudsman.org.uk/	
The Utility Warehouse	www.pinkpig.org.uk	0800 781 2707[6]

Banks

Abbey	www.abbey.com	0800 731 7774
Barclays	www.barclays.co.uk	0845 755 555
Lloyds TSB	www.lloydstsb.com	0845 0723 333
HSBC	www.hsbc.co.uk	08574 404 404
HBOS	www.hbosplc.com	0845 720 3040

Useful Websites

www.moneysaving.co.uk	for all sorts of money-saving tips
www.moneysupermarket.com	for all forms of finance and insurance.

And see the Yellow Pages for other useful numbers

---

[6] This is the author's own website.

Appendix 2
SYNOPSIS OF MONEY-SAVING IDEAS

- Close windows and doors in winter; turn heating down by three or four degrees.
- Put on warmer clothes to keep warm, do not wear summer clothes in winter and ratchet up the heating!
- Turn lights off if you are not in the room.
- Turn off TV and radio if you are not using them.
- Do not waste food: cook what you need for each day or for two or three days!
- Read the newspaper at work – why buy one when you can read it for free?
- Drive a little more slowly; it will save on your fuel bills.
- Walk when you can, rather than driving, or use a bicycle.
- Join your library instead of buying expensive novels.
- Conserve heat and hot water – bath with a friend, or shower!
- Make a bottle of wine last for more than one meal!
- Shop around for better deals on food, furniture, electronics, fuel, etc.
- Use a supplier like The Utility Warehouse for gas and electricity and telephone as they guarantee you the cheapest in the UK: see their 'triple guarantee' literature).
- Change into indoor shoes, reducing the need to clean or vacuum your carpets.
- Using a water softener or Calgon can cut down on washing and detergent costs.
- Use public transport where possible.

Appendix 3
SELECT BIBLIOGRAPHY

Ken and Kate Back, *Assertiveness at Work: A Practical Guide to Handling Awkward Situations*, McGraw-Hill Education, 1999

Edward De Bono, *Lateral Thinking: A Textbook of Creativity*, London, Penguin, 1990

Peta Lyn Farwagi, *Life Balance Programme: A Powerful Strategy for Combining Personal Fulfilment with Career Success*, Texere Publishing, 1998

Robert Fielder, Motivation

Michael Gelb, *Present Yourself*, Jalmar Books, 1988

Jerome Kern and Dorothy Fields, 'Pick Yourself Up' (song lyrics), 1936

Dr Thomas J Stanley, *Networking with the Affluent*, McGraw-Hill Education, 1997

www.ingramcontent.com/pod-product-compliance
Lightning Source LLC
Chambersburg PA
CBHW031543210526
45464CB00003B/1125